RAISED BED GARDENING FOR BEGINNERS

A Step-by-Step Guide to Growing Your Own Vegetables, Herbs, and Flowers (2023 Crash Course for Beginners)

Don Meskill

Contents

Introduction v

CAHPTER 1: Planning your Garden 1

CAHPTER 2: Location...11

CAHPTER 3: Size 15

CAHPTER 4: Best Soil for Raised Beds...........................21

CAHPTER 5: Make your Own Compost................................31

CAHPTER 6: Why People Choose the Raised Bed.............37

CAHPTER 7: Why Planting on A Raised Bed....................45

CAHPTER 8: Planting and Maintaining Crops in a Raised
Bed 53

CAHPTER 9: Crop Rotation and Planting Techniques........63

CAHPTER 10: Tips........73

CAHPTER 11: Growing and Harvesting........77

CAHPTER 12: Plant Profiles........87

CAHPTER 13: Raised Bed Maintenance........111

Conclusion........117

Introduction

Gardening is the practice of cultivating and also nurturing plants. In yards, ornamental plants are usually grown for their blooms, leaves, or overall appearance. Appearance; beneficial plants, such as origin vegetables, falling leaf vegetables, fruits, and herbs, are produced for consumption, dye use, or medicinal or aesthetic purpose. Many individuals regard horticulture to be a stress-relieving activity.

Horticulture includes anything from fruit orchards to long boulevard plantings with many types of shrubs, trees, and plants to private back gardens with grass and foundation plantings, and even container gardens planted indoors or outdoors. Horticulture may be very specialized, with just one kind of plant produced, or it can encompass a diverse variety of species in mixed cultivation. It requires active engagement in plant growth and is often labor-intensive, distinguishing it from farming or forestry.

Horticulture improves one's quality of life. It adds value to our homes, provides a sense of accomplishment and fulfillment, provides a healthy and balanced kind of amusement and leisure, or delivers the unrivaled quality of home-grown vegetables to our table. Horticulture may be natural and accomplished in little time or be regarded as a full-time pastime. Regardless of the objectives or concentration, basic knowledge of plant society and treatment concepts improves the possibilities of accomplishment and adds pleasure to the gardening experience. This website is designed for aspiring Idaho gardeners and contains basic and advanced gardening topics. It provides online connections to extensive garden information depending on location. It is a one-stop shop for individuals who desire to approach gardening with knowledge.

He is beeping horns, tires, fumes, and people running from one place to another; these are the sounds, sights, and smells that people living in cities are exposed to regularly. The one thing people overlook amid the hurry and bustle is an environmentally friendly location where they may find moments of calm and rest.

Nothing beats getting your hands in the dirt and experiencing nature, yet being one with nature is almost hard for city dwellers like Istanbulites. Blossoming, bright flowers, eco-friendly plants, and flower holders in various forms all help us change the ambiance in our homes, bringing us one step closer to the diverse hues of nature that we previously were deprived of.

Gardening has been demonstrated to offer significant health advantages and is a fantastic way for city dwellers to enjoy nature in the comfort of their own homes. For starters, it encourages people to participate in activities and duties that promote health. Gardeners who grow food organically reduce their exposure to pesticides while potentially consuming produce with increased nutritional value. Horticulture also reduces anxiety and promotes psychological health; it is considered a moderate-intensity activity that may help people live longer lives.

CHAPTER 1

Planning your Garden

Now that you've chosen to build a raised garden bed, the first step is to devise a design. Because raised garden beds tend to remain in the same place for many years, planning is essential because you won't be able to change the bed later. Planning also helps you determine how much light and water your beds will need, how big they should be, and what materials you'll use to make them.

Planning is also essential since various kinds of gardens need different things. If you want to create a raised garden bed to produce vegetables, put it somewhere that gets at least four to six hours of direct sunlight daily. On the other hand, a wildflower garden may do well in a dry place with filtered sunshine, while a Hosta garden may need a moist, shaded site.

Making plans for a raised bed garden provides you with more alternatives than you may believe. You may arrange to position your bed on a concrete patio rather than in your yard.

The following items should be included in the first phases of planning:

1. What are you going to grow? The plants you wish to cultivate will influence the placement of your garden since some need more sunshine or shade than others. As an example:

Vine Gardens - A vine garden may need a fence or trellis to climb on, so positioning the garden against the wall of your house or along the rear fence may be acceptable.

Cactus or Succulent Gardens - A succulent or cactus garden may be established in a dry, sunny site that is not readily accessible by a watering hose.

Herb or vegetable gardens need four to six hours of direct sunlight every day, consistent access to water, and simple picking by you.

2. What is your available space? You may just have enough space to build a modest raised garden bed

four feet wide by six feet long, or you may have lots of space and opt to plant many beds.

3. How big is your planting area? If you have a yard with numerous microclimates, you should be able to plant multiple garden beds with a variety of flowers, food, and attractive plants.

Consider the following factors:

Wet and Dry Zones - Do you have a damp or constantly moist part of your yard where rain collects? If this is the sole site for your garden, you may need to choose moisture-loving plants.

Is your yard often battered by hot, dry winds?

Are there a lot of shadows some or all of the time?

Will there be children or dogs in the area?

How tall will the plants you choose grow?

4. What is the objective or purpose of your garden? There are several reasons to start a garden. Knowing your unique reasons can assist you in deciding on a site and the sorts of plants to cultivate.

Food gardens may offer both nourishment and beauty for you and your family.

Formal flower gardens complement the appearance of your house and maybe a supply of one or several vibrant colors.

Wildflower beds provide a little bit of nature to your yard and attract birds, butterflies, and bees.

Perennial gardens, with minimal continuing upkeep, give long-term plant life, house enhancements, and a soothing area to spend time in for many years to come.

Design Your Bed

- Bed Border Materials

- Lining

- Bed Height

- Width

- Pathways and Access

Now that you've finished planning your garden, it's time to start creating your raised bed. There are various techniques to make a raised garden bed, but this book focuses on the simplest and easiest. We'll go through the fundamental technique, and then I'll go over a few modifications.

You must make various options while designing your garden bed. However, before you can make such selections, you need to be aware of a few facts.

Border Materials

Raised garden beds are often surrounded by wood, stone, or other retaining materials. They don't have to be, but when you make a container-style bed, you may boost the height so that your plants are easier to reach. Having an enclosed bed also enables you to dig deeper into the dirt, giving your plants plenty of area for their roots.

Some border material suggestions:

- Railroad Ties - While old railroad ties are a popular option for making a garden bed border, you should avoid putting them in a food garden if they've been treated with chemicals.

- Kits - Most nurseries and home and garden shops sell pre-cut wood and plastic kits.

- Logs - If you have a lot of fallen trees in your region, you may use them to make lovely garden bed borders.

- Stones and Rocks - If you have many rocks lying about, they may also be used to build lovely garden beds.

- Bricks or Blocks - Red bricks and concrete blocks can form lovely garden beds and may survive for a long time.

Bed Lining

Material may also be used to line the bottom and sides of a raised garden bed. This is entirely optional and is mainly dependent on the location of your bed.

The lining is essential when making the bed in an area where there are moles or other digging ground creatures since it prevents them from entering your garden from beneath. The lining is essential when establishing a plant bed on a patio. If you intend to build your garden bed on a concrete patio or a wood deck, for example, you risk damaging the patio or deck over time. Without a liner, your garden's soil, water, and fertilizer may flow out the bottom. This might discolor or break the concrete, causing the hardwood deck to degrade.

Hardware cloth is handy if you are using a lining to keep critters from burrowing into your garden from the bottom. This is a metal substance that has the appearance of a window screen.

Use a pond liner or thick plastic to protect garden surfaces.

You may omit the liner if you're not worried about digging rats and will create the garden bed on top of an existing grass or bare soil location. By not placing a liner in your bed, water will be allowed to run down through the existing soil, and you will not have to worry about your plants being waterlogged. Worms may be able to enter your garden from below over time, which is beneficial since it helps maintain the soil quality in your garden bed.

Height of the bed

The materials you choose to build your bed will influence its height to some degree. Alternatively, you may choose border materials that will help you achieve your desired height first, then choose your chosen height.

Raised garden beds may be just a few inches higher than the surrounding ground. However, they must be at least eight to ten inches tall in order for little plants to have enough place for their roots. Many gardeners choose to build taller beds, so they don't have to bend down as much while caring for their plants.

You may design your own garden beds to be whatever height you like. The standard depth is one to two feet, although there are no restrictions that indicate you can't go higher.

Choose the height you want depending on your physical demands, bearing in mind the initial expense of filling the bed with dirt in mind.

Bed Width

Raised vegetable beds should be no more than three to four feet wide. This breadth allows you to easily reach the middle of your bed from all sides.

Because I am short, I like garden beds that are three feet broad. I'm five feet tall. I can reach the middle of a four-foot-wide bed, but it's a little stretch that becomes weary after a while. Three-foot beds are also recommended when one side is inaccessible. If you build a garden bed against a fence, for example, you won't be able to stroll around to the far side since the fence will block that side.

Four feet is a perfect width if you have the room, are tall enough, and your mattresses can be accessible from all four corners. Raised garden beds may be constructed to match your unique area and requirements and can be as little as one or two feet wide.

Pathways and Access

As previously said, you must be able to quickly reach the garden beds that you plant. Even if you cultivate low-maintenance perennials or cacti, you must eradicate weeds, cover areas with mulch, apply compost, and regularly deadhead blooms. All of these operations need plant access.

Pathways and access spaces are essential for establishing bed layouts, placements, sizes, and style. The first important thing to ask oneself is, "How much access do I require?"

If you want to have one or more garden beds along a fence at the rear of your yard, you won't need to bother establishing paths since the space directly in front of your beds will be the principal access point by default. If, on the other hand, you have a 50-by-30-foot yard and want to have various beds throughout, you will need to carefully plan your access pathways.

The roads between your garden beds may be broad enough to accommodate a full-sized wheelbarrow or garden cart or just wide enough for comfortable strolling. For tiny walkways, 18 inches is a decent size. This allows you to move about without sacrificing too much of your growing area.

Grab a piece of paper and jot down your particular selections now that you know what decisions must be taken to create your garden bed. You may either draw a quick sketch of your ideas or use a spreadsheet tool on your computer to help you visualize your goals.

1. Mark the location of each of your garden beds.

2. Take note of the dimensions of each bed.

3. Label the paths and access points with their sizes and locations.

4. Make a list of the materials you'll need for the bed borders.

5. Make a note of the sort of lining you want to use if any.

With these specifics in hand, it's time to gather the necessary supplies.

CHAPTER 2

Location

Pairing the appropriate plants with the appropriate raised bed location is critical. If you have a tiny garden, you may not have as many alternatives in terms of space. Still, there are many plants that may fit certain elements and areas of the garden, such as the shaded region, the moist environment, or even dry soil. All you have to do is choose the best plant to fit into the available area.

Your garden's shady spots

Plants, in general, need sunshine for metabolism and food synthesis. It is also essential that they get enough of it to develop. You don't have to be discouraged if your little garden is situated in an area with little or no sunshine. There are alternative plants that may be planted in such areas. There are plants that thrive in the shadow. You may use them in this area. Leafy crops such as cabbage, spinach, and summer salads are examples of these plants. Shade is ideal for all these plants since they like a cool climate. Because of the abundant shade, their bedding will virtually never dry. This will provide an appropriate cold temperature for the root system. Other decorative plants that flourish in shaded areas of the garden include hostas, ferns, epimediums, and hellebores.

Take note of the light's path.

One of the things I examine before building a raised bed is the direction of the sunlight and how the area accommodates it. This is especially important in tiny gardens that are tucked between walls. It should be noted that certain plants that are still developing may grow out of the sunlight once they reach a specific height. Taller plants may also unexpectedly obstruct an area and prevent it from receiving sunlight.

You should survey your property to determine where the sun shines the most throughout the day. Raised beds built in such areas will naturally be warmer and brighter due to the consistent sunshine they get. This is great since each raised bed should get maximum sunshine.

Don't only look at locations with the most sunshine. Consider the spacing of the sun-filled place as well. Look for the biggest area in your complex where the sun shines the brightest.

Take into account the present weather conditions when doing so. Remember that the sun is significantly higher in the summer sky than in the fall and winter. Check whether your garden still gets sunshine at its lowest height if you want to prolong the season.

Cut down overhanging and overgrown foliage and branches to let more light into the garden. If you have neighbors who have trees in their gardens that have over-grown and are interfering with the light reception in your garden, you might ask them to cut them back a bit for your benefit. The height of your fence might sometimes interfere with the receiving of sunlight. You may lower it to let more sunshine in, but this will cost you some privacy.

Where to Plant a Raised Bed Garden

This is something I believe you should take into serious consideration while planning your garden. If the garden includes veggies or other herbs, you should strive to position it as near to the kitchen as feasible. I've discovered that this allows me to quickly rush in and out of the kitchen and plug in one or two vegetables. You should also consider your neighbors' privacy. To gain seclusion, I previously increased the height of my garden bed borders. You may do this or put the bed on a patio or a sitting bed. If you intend to grow tall trees in your garden, keep them away from the windows, so they don't obscure your view of the garden.

Providing Protection Against Elemental Forces

Plants, like humans, need shelter and protection from the weather. When plants are subjected to excessive wind, they decimate and begin to fall off because wind causes plants to dry up and drains moisture from the earth.

Plants seldom pollinate amid severe winds because most pollinators cannot endure the conditions. I strive to give adequate wind shelter for my crops whenever I plant them. To keep the winds at bay, I encircle them with hedges, walls, and fences. I observed that hedges are the best kind of windbreakers; however, they are semi-permeable since they allow some sort of wind circulation.

Other windbreakers, like fences, may completely prevent wind from reaching the plants, but they can also be harmful in that overly powerful gusts can buffer along the top edge and drop down into the raised bed with increased force.

CHAPTER 3

Size

Now that you've decided to build your raised bed garden, you must be eager to start. Unfortunately, starting immediately necessitates planning and settling on the raised bed specs. So, although it's not quite a time to get your hands filthy, it doesn't mean you can't have much fun with this procedure.

You will need to make crucial decisions that will significantly impact how your raised bed garden looks, feels, and works. One of these aspects is the size of the beds you will be elevating. There is no one correct solution for the size; it is totally up to you. However, it is critical to understand how size affects the garden's function. Similarly, you'll need to pick what material to employ for the bed's frame. Again, this is your option, so we'll look at a variety of materials to weigh the advantages and drawbacks of each. Finally, selecting a design is critical. A raised garden bed does not have to have a rectangular shape. You'll find a plethora of raised bed garden ideas to replicate or use as inspiration for your own. Regarding this phase, the only restriction is your creativity, which makes it so much fun.

Big Garden Bed or Small Garden Bed: Which is Better?

When it comes to size, we must first consider width and height. The amount of space available in the garden will decide the length. You may have an indefinite raised garden bed (if you have the space). This endless bed could produce pretty effectively as long as it had adequate height for the plant roots and a narrow enough width for you to monitor and care for each plant. Because length does not need to be considered when determining size, we may dismiss any worries regarding that variable.

With width and height in hand, we can consider whether it is preferable to be large or small. The answer is a bit more nuanced in that the best response is "either." The main issue with the size is not being too large or too small, but too big or too small. Regarding size, the prob-lem regions are at either extreme of the size chart (tiny or vast), while the center portion (small or giant) is ideal for your raised garden bed. Let's begin with breadth.

If your raised garden bed is too narrow, you may not be able to grow your plants. It's simple to see a garden bed with a narrow width and know that your plants won't fit, so this isn't a common issue for gardeners. The more prevalent problem has a raised garden bed that is too broad. This is the gardening counterpart of the saying, "Eyes bigger than the stomach." While the equation "more space equals more plants" is theoretically correct, it ignores the reality that you must still care for those plants. You won't be able to reach the plants in the center of a broad raised bed if there is too much room for you to reach over. As a result, neglected plants and indicators of illness or infestation go undetected until it's too late. So, how can we ensure that our raised beds aren't overly broad?

If you have access to all four sides, keeping them no broader than four feet across is the best rule of thumb. If you have a garden bed with a side you can't get to because it's up against your home, for example, you should remove a foot. If you go larger, you may not have any trouble reaching the plants in the center when everything is still a seedling. However, when their foliage matures and the bed fills up, reaching those difficult-to-reach plants becomes much more difficult. Keep in mind that this is an average based on most people's height and reach. You should reduce your breadth by half a foot if you are shorter. Taller gardeners may get away with increasing the width somewhat, but this may be a problem if you need to travel away and have someone look over your garden.

Height is a simpler calculation to do. A raised bed typically ranges in height from half a foot to three feet. However, since we're talking about mattresses with a bottom, we should stay at least a foot in height. The more dirt you have put on a bed, the taller it is. Your plants' roots will extend out into that soil in quest of nourishment. A mesh bottom would be required for a smaller bed in the half-foot range to prevent pests from reaching your plants from below while still allowing the roots access to the natural dirt underneath. So we need a high enough bed, so the roots do not run out of room. At the very least, that's a foot. If you intend on growing a lot in the raised bed, you may want to go even higher.

Going taller will have a variety of implications. For starters, it will improve drainage in the bed. However, it will retain moisture for a more extended period of time. As a result, the water will drain away from the roots faster, but since there is more soil to drain through, the bed will retain moisture for longer. This implies that the higher the bed, the less it has to be watered. This is especially beneficial since most raised garden beds have wooden frames, and the more they are exposed to water, the faster they degrade and must be replaced.

Keep in mind that the dirt within will be pushing it outwards when it comes to the wooden frame. That is, the dirt does not just desire to remain in place; gravity is constantly pressing on it, causing it to spill everything. As a result, the dirt in the bed exerts pressure on the frame. The greater the pressure, the higher the bed. A weaker wood may be adequate for a foot-tall garden bed, but the pressure of a three-foot-tall bed may fracture the wood and pour all over your yard. The thicker the wood that must be utilized, the higher the bed. Other materials, such as concrete, may be employed, but they will provide their own set of challenges.

So, the key to creating the ideal raised garden bed size is to keep it at least a foot high and no more than four feet broad. You are free to do anything you want after that. Just keep in mind that more dirt means a tremendous strain on the frame, in terms of frames.

CHAPTER 4

Best Soil for Raised Beds

Best Soil Recommendations for Your Raised Bed Garden

One advantage of a raised bed garden is that you can manage the soil that goes into it. This hastens the plant's development. Compost combined with clay or sand is the most excellent soil advice for your garden.

Clay has several advantages for organic gardening that no other material can, and the results are priceless when combined with compost. This may not only be used to feed plants but it can also be used to combat pests. There are various advantages that clay has for greens, mainly when used as soil.

Clay contains several essential elements and metals that plants need to grow. These are not found in many other soils. Iron, calcium, potassium, and even tiny quantities of other chemical molecules are among the nutrients it contains. It may also increase the potency of the compost.

Clay particles are negatively charged, which allows them to attract and absorb positively charged substances such as ammonium, magnesium, calcium, and other trace elements. Clay is particularly fertile due to its capacity to absorb ample nutrients for plants.

Compost has a vital function in clay management. The fact that humified compost contains minimal oxidizable carbon and accessible nitrogen makes it resistant to decomposition. Compost is necessary because it increases organic carbon as well as humic matter, which helps to enhance the physical qualities of the soil over time.

The usage of compost may also attract earthworms and other helpful microbes by providing them with a nutritious meal. The existence of creatures and even bacteria indicates this is a healthy substance.

It is well-recognized that they reflect a balanced environment. These are required to work the soil naturally by decomposing organic materials and releasing nutrients as it moves through the ground. Compost-enriched soil may undoubtedly aid in managing disease and insect concerns that threaten the garden. When compost is used, the pH of the ground changes as well.

The combination of clay and compost may bring various advantages that no other combination can. If compost is used, it will bond to clay particles, generating considerably bigger particles with a lot greater air gap immediately between them. These holes may allow for significantly improved surface water drainage and even air penetration.

Gardening using organic materials, such as this mix, is a more ecologically responsible option. But that's not all; since the materials used are widely accessible, this is also a cost-effective way. Because you can make your own compost, the only item you'll need to buy is clay. When these two elements mix, they provide the perfect soil for your raised bed garden.

The Best Raised Bed Soil Mix

Your raised bed soil mix will be determined by what is available and your budget. In a moment, I'll tell you what many people believe to be the ideal soil mix for containers or raised beds, but at the end of the day, you may use whatever works for you. The optimal blend will not be inexpensive, and if you are filling a large number of beds, it may become prohibitively costly. Whatever method you use, the goal is to have lots of nutrients in the soil for your plants to thrive effectively.

Most of my raised beds are made of compost (both handmade and store-bought), soil from other areas of the allotment, manure, leftover compost from pots and grow bags, and purchased topsoil and manure.

This is entirely due to financial constraints, but I would absolutely add more variation to the mix in an ideal world. If I prepare ahead of time, I will fill the bed with manure, cover it, and leave it for six to nine months, turning it over regularly until it has completely decomposed.

Again, the specific composition of your soil will be determined by what you are growing. The above-pictured bed contains around 50% horse dung, which will have decomposed wonderfully by spring; therefore, this bed will most likely end up housing pumpkins since they are voracious eaters. If I were planting blueberries in the bed, I would add ericaceous compost or pine needle mulch to make the soil more acidic. The benefit of raised bed gardening is that you can change the soil based on your planting!

Before you begin amending the soil, you must first understand what you are dealing with. How excellent is the soil in your beds right now? If the soil is excellent enough, you may increase the soil level by utilizing dirt transported from other locations (for example, digging a pond and using that material), compost, or purchased soil. If you're creating raised beds because the soil in your location is poor, you'll need to bring in all the soil and compost.

If you reside in a region with thick clay soil, you may break it up by digging in lots of organic debris and some horticultural sand. After a few growing seasons, the clay will be much looser, and you'll have eight to twelve inches of healthy soil. If your soil is sandy, add organic matter and topsoil to improve the quality of the soil. You will need to be patient since this procedure might take many years.

Remember that you want your soil to have a healthy, loose consistency that is rich in nutrients and simple to dig or weed. This bed has been cleaned and has had some handmade compost added to it, resulting in a wonderful soft loam that will be ideal for growing veggies.

You must consider what you will plant in the beds since this will impact how you modify the soil. Make the soil more acidic for acid-loving plants, or cover it with shredded pine needles or branches. If necessary, you may simply alter the soil in a bed between seasons, but keep in mind that the pH level takes many months to change.

If you're curious about the pH of your soil (which might explain why certain crops fail on a regular basis), you can purchase pH testing kits online or at local garden shops to find out. Most plants prefer soil that is near neutral in pH, while other plants prefer more acidic or alkaline soil. If your soil is excessively acidic or alkaline, you may have trouble producing even the most basic crops and need to be amended. Most veggies like a pH range of 6.0 to 7.0. Adding five pounds of lime to 100 square feet of soil will elevate the pH level by one.

It is cheaper to purchase dirt in bulk for your raised beds, and you must acquire screened topsoil. This is sterilized soil, so you can be certain that no bugs or other issues will be brought into your beds. You may frequently acquire free dirt from neighbors who have completed gardening efforts but be mindful that this soil may include weeds, bugs, illnesses, stones, and who knows what else. However, it is free, which is a significant factor for many people, especially when installing many raised beds!

Purchasing dirt and compost in bulk can save you a lot of money. It is often purchased by the ton and delivered in bulk bags, so you will need access for the delivery truck to dump them down in your garden or be prepared to go back and forth with your wheelbarrow while filling the raised beds! You may find some fantastic prices if you shop around. You can sometimes save money by purchasing dirt loose rather than in bags, but this may be messier, which some people dislike.

Combine your topsoil with an equal amount of home-made compost, mushroom compost, or manure. You may combine it on a tarp or lay it on your bed and mix it there. When I began filling my beds, I would pour in a wheelbarrow of soil, then a wheelbarrow of compost, and then mix the two together, continuing the procedure until the bed was full. Then, twice or three times a week, I'd give the bed a quick fork over to maintain mixing it up and breaking up any clumps (horse dung clumps stops decaying, especially in rainy weather). You must keep the soil aerated so that the microorganisms that break down the manure do not suffocate and can perform their job.

If you really want to go all out, but it won't be inexpensive, the finest soil combination to utilize is made up of one-third of each of the following:

Vermiculite, perlite, or coconut coir are all options.

Moss made with peat

Different composts (a variety of store-bought/homemade composts that contain a diverse range of micronutrients)

This outstanding soil mix guarantees that your plants will develop exceptionally well since it is free draining while keeping the moisture, and it is filled with critical nutrients for healthy plants. This mix is most typically used in pots, although it allows for considerably denser planting in raised beds.

Filling tall raised beds with dirt might be costly if you are creating them! If you know you're going to plant shallow-rooted plants (e.g., salad veggies, onions), you may fill the bottom half with empty plastic bottles, rocks, stones, or anything similar to save on soil. Simply cover this inert substance with landscaping cloth to aid drainage and prevent too much soil from vanishing between the filler. It will save you a lot of money when making waist-high raised beds.

If you really want dirt in your bed, you may utilize what is known as the lasagna approach, which will be discussed more below. Fill your raised bed with layers of leaves or grass clippings (but not too thick as it will mat), straw (not hay as it contains seeds), shredded bark, or wood chips until you are six to twelve inches from the top. These biodegradable layers will decompose over time and generate beautiful rich soil, but in the interim, they will help you save money!

Over this biodegradable material, place a layer of untreated cardboard, removing any tape and staples. Fill the remainder of the bed with your soil mix.

The following year, the soil layer will have decreased where the material on the bottom has decomposed, allowing you to add a new layer of compost to the top. Later, the original filler material will have broken down, allowing you to flip the bed over.

CHAPTER 5

Make your Own Compost

Any herb planter will benefit from adding vitamins and natural soil nutrients to help plants grow effectively. Compost is one of the most well-known and valuable items to add. Compost may be purchased at any nursery supply store, but preparing your own is easy (and less expensive). Whether your nursery is inside or outside, compost will help all of your herbs grow better.

What Exactly Is Composting?

Composting is shown by putting natural materials near water in a heap or container. This heap is switched on and off, and the beneficial microorganisms thrive. This generates a lot of heat and separates the raw natural components into a dull, rich, soil-like substance. There will be no distinguishing features, and the finished compost will have a fresh, natural aroma.

How Much Compost Will You Require?

If you have a small indoor nursery, you may produce less compost. You can never have enough of this dark gold if you grow your herbs outdoors. An excellent idea for indoor composting is to get a plastic tub that fits under your kitchen sink and start composting with night crawlers. This is known as vermiculture, and it is the best way to generate compost for all of your indoor plants.

You may need to put your compost heap in a container for more significant amounts. These may be fashioned of any material you can think of. You may make use of wooden beds. Simply connect three beds and leave the fourth side free for turning. These bed receptacles are not difficult to shift in the fall and have enough area to easily combine the material. There are several designs of compost canisters to choose from. You may spend a lot of money on an expensive version that is just a barrel with a handle to twist it around with. The choice is entirely yours. Now, onto the fixings essential for a healthy compost heap.

How Is Compost Made?

The magic of compost requires three essential elements:

- Green substance

- Darker fabric

- sufficient dampness

The green substance has a lot of nitrogen. Examples of kitchen waste include espresso beans, peelings, organic product centers, and eggshells. Any non-oily or meaty kitchen waste may be composted. Green materials include compost (not canine or feline excrement, but just farm animal waste), grass clippings, leaves, and weeds.

Carbon content is higher in darker materials. This category includes paper, sawdust, small branches and twigs, and straw. You may not believe the things have anything to give your compost, but they do. The proportion of nitrogen to carbon should ideally be equal parts each. Cornstalks and kitchen waste may also be used. Every component contributes to the overall picture.

Water is the last essential fixing in a thriving compost heap. Your heap will take a long time to accomplish anything without wetness and, if properly dry, will not separate by any stretch of the imagination. If your heap is too damp, it will stink and grow nasty when the percentage of awful tiny creatures surpasses the great. You want it to be damp but not dripping wet. If you don't receive enough precipitation to accomplish the task, pour a can over it once a week to get things rolling. If the core of your compost heap becomes heated, you'll know it's working well. This is critical for disinfecting the compost and killing any weed seeds or other illnesses that may be present. The warmth is proof that the percentage is beneficial to your compost heap.

What Else Must You Do With Your Compost Pile?

You will bring your heap in from the outdoors roughly once a week. This doesn't have to be anything huge; just scoop the outside of the heap toward the inside and keep moving the heap until you have updated it so fresh compost is exposed. As a result, all favorable critters may have a chance to chip away at all of the heap's fixes. If your heap heats up, becomes moist, and is regularly rotated, you should have dull, bright compost in roughly one to two months.

Presently What?

Use this prolific growth on any herbs you have, whether indoors or outside. Include a lot of it in the soil you intend to plant in the spring. Use it all season to finish off any soil compacted due to water overflow or settling. Separate your nursery in the autumn and save any bits that are not harmful. Put another compost heap to work throughout winter, and you'll have fresh compost to use in the spring.

Finally, keep in mind that composting is an ongoing side interest. It's not something you accomplish in 14 days and then forget about for a year. Maintain an off-the-beaten-path heap of this "black treasure," and always have a place to repurpose a lot of your family unit garbage and change it into something worthwhile.

CHAPTER 6

Why People Choose the Raised Bed

We will look at the several advantages of growing plants on a raised bed rather than in the ground. These factors vary from the amount of space they take up to the health of the plants, the influence it has on the human body, how it changes the qualities of the soil, and how it reduces the amount of effort required to care for your plants.

People have started to employ raised beds in their gardens for these (and other!) reasons. But before we get into the advantages, let's explain what we mean by "raised bed gardening."

What exactly is Raised Bed Gardening?

There is no definitive definition for the phrase. Raised beds may come in a variety of sizes, styles, and designs that are all distinct from one another. Rather, the phrase should be seen as a broad category into which many various methods of gardening may be classified. Consider it almost like a movie genre. You have action movies, but there are vehicle and martial arts movies. They are all unique, yet they all have some characteristics.

From the phrase itself, we may deduce some information. The fact that we are discussing a raised bed implies that we are putting our seeds above ground level. It is up to the individual grower to decide how much they want to go above ground level. Your raised bed could be a few feet from the ground, but this isn't always the case. If you've ever seen a flower bed affixed to a windowsill, you've seen another kind of raised bed. Windowsill beds are often placed at waist level (on the low end) or chest level (on the high end). So, although the height varies greatly, one thing we can all agree on is that the bed is elevated above the ground.

Another element that is shared by all types of raised beds is the presence of a frame. Whatever material the frame is built of, it aims to keep the growing environment within the bed distinct from the natural world outside it. This frame is filled with healthy soil, and the frame's walls keep it from leaking out. Many gardeners pick sites that offer them access to all four sides of their raised bed; however, this is not a characteristic of the raised bed itself but rather a consequence of the gardener's design decisions. Raised beds next to windowsills do not have this capability, although it does not exclude them from becoming raised beds.

While a frame is common, it does not always require a bottom. Many include a bottom to further segregate the developing environment from the outside world; however, this is unnecessary. However, a bottom will assist in keeping pests out of your garden, so we'll treat the raised beds as if they had one.

As a result, the primary qualities we will use to identify and discuss raised bed gardens throughout the rest of the book may be divided into three categories. These are beds that are one or two feet above ground level. They are intended to provide a distinct growth environment over which the gardener has complete control and which is isolated from the natural world. Finally, these raised beds include a frame along the sides and bottom to hold everything in place. When all three of these characteristics are present, you have a raised bed garden.

So, now that we've established this description let's move on to the subject of why you'd want to work with a raised bed in the first place.

The Advantages of Raised Bed Gardening

There are several advantages to utilizing a raised bed to cultivate your plants. These vary from those that help the plants to those that benefit the environment and those that directly benefit the gardener. You may not be interested in all of them, but there are so many that you will undoubtedly gravitate toward some of them.

Beds on Wheels Reduce the amount of space required for growth: A raised bed works like a regular plant container does. That is, it enables you to grow a plant in a considerably smaller area than is generally necessary while growing in nature. If you have a lot of space in your yard to grow plants, this method works well when planting straight into the ground. However, if you have limited room, a raised bed may be just what you need to plant everything you desire. Raised beds enable gardeners to maintain their plants in a single area, eliminating the need to build rows, as is common when planting crops. You can grow many more plants in the same area since you can completely circle around a raised bed or at least don't have to go through it at any time. Furthermore, a raised bed garden does not need to be planted in soil, to begin with. You might start a raised bed garden on top of a concrete parking lot since the grower fills a raised bed with soil.

Raised Beds Look Great: While not a benefit in and of itself, this feature contributes to the overall aesthetic of your garden. Because you may customize the material, shape, size, and style of the raised bed frame, you have almost endless options for how your raised beds will appear. Many people use wooden frames and don't give them much thought. In contrast, others embellish their frames, using materials like solidified clay or concrete and pairing them with certain plants and flowers to highlight the beauty of the plants themselves. Others are less concerned with how the frames complement the plants and more concerned with how the frames enhance the overall appearance of their landscaping. Raised beds may therefore serve as both a valuable means to cultivate your plants and a decorative approach to embellish your yard.

You don't have to bend as far: While gardening is a popular pastime for many people worldwide, many say that the most challenging part is all of the bending required to maintain the garden. To plant your seeds, you must kneel down and gently cover them with dirt. Then, if you want to trim your plants, you'll have to do some additional bending. Do you need to look for pests? That requires more bending. Have you seen a weed that needs to be removed? You can bet you're bending again. It's finally harvest time. More bending is required. Those who are young and healthy may not think twice about it, but older gardeners and those with terrible backs are all too familiar with the throbbing ache and aching muscles that this causes. Raised bed gardening is one method to prevent this suffering. While some raised beds are barely a foot height, there's no reason you couldn't design yours to be waist or chest level so you can care for your plants without leaning over.

Raised Bed Gardens Do Not Require Tilling: Another way raised bed gardens to save you from tired muscles is that no tilling is required. You must till the soil between crops when growing plants in the ground. Tilling is the process of turning, excavating, or stirring soil. This is done to help maintain the soil beautiful and healthy since the recently harvested plants sucked up all the nutrients they could locate in the soil with their roots. Large-scale agricultural operations employ specialized machines to till the soil, while smaller gardens need human labor with shovels, rakes, and other tools. Raised bed gardens do not need tilling between seasons. Instead, fertilizer, compost, or manure is put into the soil to offer the nutrients your plants require. Not only will this save you time and work, but the act of tilling soil may actually damage the quality of the soil, so by eliminating the tilling process, you are actually extending the amount of time your raised bed garden can go before having to be replaced with a new combination.

Gardening on Raised Beds Get Rid of Pests: Pests in this context relate to the bothersome small insects that seek to eat your plants and more giant animals such as deer, which may swiftly devastate you a garden if not recognized early. Slugs and snails will be able to get into your garden, but they are sluggish movers, and if you are vigilant and keep a watch on your garden, you should be able to knock them off before they get into the bed itself. Because we are treating raised bed gardens as though they had a bottom to the frame, pests such as moles and groundhogs will be unable to enter the garden from the bottom. Deer may be troublesome, but some simple netting around the raised bed can keep them from poking their noses in. Winged insects such as whiteflies, certain aphid species, and male scales will be the most bothersome. It is almost hard to prevent these little pests from entering your raised bed garden. Still, simple preventive treatments, such as neem oil sprays, may help reduce infestation frequency, and thoughtful management will enable you to notice them early before they become a severe issue.

Raised beds allow the soil to drain more effectively: Raised beds are an alternative for gardeners who want to cultivate in places prone to floods. This is crucial to understand since plants have an unusual interaction with water. Water is one of the most crucial elements they need to develop correctly, and it is critical that you constantly offer sufficient of it to your plants. However, too much water might drown the roots of your plants and cause them to decay. When root rot takes hold, it may swiftly spread to the plant's stem and leaves, killing it in no time. As a result, you must utilize well-draining soil to keep your plants healthy. However, one way to modify any soil's drainage speed is to elevate it. The greater the elevation, the more space water has to escape. Elevating the level of the soil is really advised for plants like succulents when grown in the ground. Still, by raising our garden beds, we achieve the same effect, and it enables us to maintain our plants free of rot without doing any further precautions.

CHAPTER 7

Why Planting on A Raised Bed

Is it correct to declare you're trying to figure out how to plant your nursery this year? Perhaps you've heard that many people are turning to elevated nursery beds instead of traditional nursery methods. They are doing this for some fantastic reasons. Right now, we'll go over ten reasons why you should choose raised bed gardening for your plants this year.

Nursery Boxes vs. Raised Beds Raised beds are sometimes referred to as nursery boxes by certain people. Elevated beds are just dirt raised above the surrounding soil and surrounded by an edge constructed of wood, pebbles, solid squares, or other imaginative solutions. Raised beds are not the same as nursery growers. Growers are high holders with bottoms to prevent dirt from falling out. There are no bottoms to raised beds.

1. **Less Stress**

One significant benefit of using elevated nursery beds is that you put less pressure on your back and knees. Who wouldn't want this advantage? This is because raised beds are worked with dividers that are, in any case, 6 in. to 1 ft. high, removing the need for you to twist around while you operate in your nursery. If you build your beds with four-foot sides, you will find it much easier to work in your nursery.

I prefer using construction materials that are a few inches thick as well so that we can have a genuinely open sitting area. We can pick weeds, monitor vegetable progress, and plant strength while sitting comfortably rather than slouching over. This will make working in your nursery a lot more enjoyable, especially if you have versatility issues.

When it comes to nursery beds, you may be really creative. You may raise your mattresses to standing height if necessary. A few tables have been turned into plant beds. You can even add wheels to make them portable. Be creative and do what is comfortable for you. Obviously, some may argue that they are growers rather than garden beds. It's completely meaningless. There are no bottoms on raised nursery beds.

2. Possibility

Everyone, no matter where they reside, may start a nursery with elevated nursery beds. Raised bed gardening is rapidly gaining popularity as people realize that you don't need acres of productive land to run a lucrative nursery. In any case, whether open-air space is limited or you just approach a clean area, elevated nursery beds may now be an effective plant specialist.

I wish I had considered nursery beds when I was trying to establish a nursery in our hard treat dirt in Utah many years ago. I would have been much more productive if I had used them instead of fighting the unfriendly pastry dirt. The key to using garden beds on asphalt is to ensure that they are level, do not get soggy, and have enough natural matter to absorb water. Mulch is also an essential component of every nursery bed. Mulch options include straw, feed, wood chips, and pine bark. The mulch will smother weeds and preserve moisture in the soil.

Obviously, the optimal situation for raised nursery beds is to be placed on exposed soil. If you are expanding on hard surfaces, for example, concrete or asphalt, ensure that the profundity of your nursery beds is at least 18 in. This gives the roots adequate room to grow and be healthy. The profundity of a raised nursery bed based on exposed soil does not have to be so deep since the roots may also extend out into the ground soil.

3. Planting Early

By early spring, most farmers are eager to get their seeds into the ground. If you reside in a cold climate, such as the northern parts of the United States, you may be employed during a short growing season. In Idaho, for example, the developing season is estimated to last 167 days. In comparison, portions of California are predicted to have roughly 300 days of development time. That is a significant difference, so you can see why early planting is appealing!

The earth becomes cemented in the winter and requires a long time to warm up. A remarkable feature of nursery beds is that the earth in them is often hotter than ground soil, implying earlier planting and a more extended nursery season. This is fantastic news if you live in an area with a short growing season and want to start your nursery earlier in the spring!

Soil that has compacted throughout the winter will need some effort to heat up. From the start, the operation is mild. Raised beds with a decent soil construction will deplete productively and retain the sun's warmth. That is why elevated nursery beds allow you to start your nursery earlier than traditional nurseries.

Solid plants, such as lettuce, radish, and peas, may be planted when the soil temperature is consistently 44.5°F (7°C). You may also try using dark plastic to help warm up the dirt and dry it off a little. One piece of advice is to position your nursery beds so that they take advantage of the midday light and are not obscured by trees or other buildings.

4. Fewer Weeds

That is all someone has to know! I'm all in! Raised nursery beds reduce the number of weeds you need to pick during nursery season. There are many causes for this, but the main one is due to the construction of the nursery bed. Please allow me to explain. You begin by cleaning the area where your nursery bed will be placed. This entails, at the very least, removing any grasses and weeds from the topsoil. It is preferable if the earth is worked 18 inches and vibrations are also evacuated.

Regardless of whether they start with a pristine surface, many people choose to place papers, cardboard, scene texture, or equipment material beneath their infant bed to protect anything from becoming back. In the long term, the papers and cardboard will decay and provide nutrients to your plants.

Nursery beds are subsequently filled with nutrient-rich soil, and any weeds that do emerge may be efficiently plucked since the ground is so nice and free. Remember that removing any weeds that do grow up will not break your spirit since you are not slouching down on the ground to reach them. Win, win, win!

5. Rat Control

What rodents are you used to that tunnel beneath your nursery and damage your vegetables? This category includes a variety of rodents. Voles, Moles, Gophers, Ground Squirrels, and other ground-dwelling rats are on the list. Raised nursery beds are an excellent way to keep rats at bay.

This requires a little forethought on your side when organizing your nursery beds, but it's simple. To ensure it, I'd recommend placing chicken wire at the base of the bed before filling it with dirt and expanding a few crawls beyond the bed. If you are unfamiliar with dealing with burrowing rats, you should skip this step. However, if this is your first time gardening or you are considering another region, I strongly advise you to be proactive and lay chicken wire around the base of your nursery bed.

In hindsight, you would not want to have to remove your mattresses in order to install wiring. That might lead to a lengthy treatment.

EasyGardenBox
Dealer
RAISED BED
GARDEN BOX
4'X4'

CHAPTER 8

Planting and Maintaining Crops in a Raised Bed

This chapter is for you if you haven't decided what you want to plant in your raised bed garden yet. Several solutions are accessible, but the critical limiting element is your local climate. You won't be able to cultivate plants that need a lot of sunlight if you don't have much of it and instead live in a cooler climate. However, once you get over this hurdle, you'll discover that many plants thrive in a raised bed.

A raised garden bed is similar to a standard garden bed but with some extra advantages, such as more significant drainage. If you can grow it in the ground in your location, you can grow it in a raised bed garden. Some plants, however, thrive on elevated beds rather than the ground. Succulents are one such example. These plants are native to hot and arid climates and like highly sandy soil, even to the point of becoming rocky. While too much moisture will damage the roots of almost any plant, succulents are particularly susceptible. The increased drainage speed provided by elevating a garden bed for succulents will allow them to live and grow much more easily than if simply planted in the ground. If you're going to plant succulents at all, I highly recommend either a raised bed or an elevated spot in the ground.

Conversely, succulents are only one (wonderful) example of what you may plant in a raised garden bed. This chapter has several others ranging from flowers to vegetables and everything in between.

Planting Out Your Raised Bed

There are many factors to consider when picking what to plant in your raised bed. Among them are the following:

How many raised beds must you plant? More than one bed allows for greater production of a single vegetable kind.

How large is your family, and how many people do you plan to feed?

Is your raised bed exposed to direct sunlight for at least 6-8 hours every day?

What are your favorite foods? This may seem foolish, but it is really simple to develop anything just because you can. Only to discover that everything is squandered at the end of the season because you dislike Brussels sprouts, for example!

Did you grow anything on this bed last year if you used it? Crop rotation is essential for a successful harvest.

As you may have guessed, what to plant is a question with several solutions based on your own desires and requirements - as well as the wants and needs of your friends and neighbors!

As a result, I'll go through a few various planting regimens to inspire you to come up with your own.

Crop types

To begin, we must separate the crops into their distinct families in order to get the most out of the soil conditions in which they are planted.

Root Vegetables: Carrots, potatoes, parsnips, beets, fennel, and celery

Cabbage, Brussels sprouts, cauliflower, broccoli, radish, and swede turnip are all brassicas.

Peas, mange tout, French, and broad beans are examples of legumes.

Alliums (family of onions): onions, garlic, chives, and leeks

Aubergine, potato, tomato, peppers, and eggplant are all members of the Solanaceae family.

Cucurbits include cucumber, squash, pumpkin, melon, and marrow.

Miscellaneous: All fruits, lettuce, herbs, sweetcorn, chicory, and asparagus

Though by no means exhaustive, this list provides a solid selection of the most widely cultivated veggies and is more than enough to get started with!

Watch your height

One of the essential things to remember is to keep an eye on the height of the plants. Plant the tall plants or climbers near the north end of the bed to avoid shading the remainder of your crop from the all-important life-giving sunshine.

In other words, if you have a raised bed that faces the sun for most of the day, a frame constructed along the back of the bed would be a smart option. This allows you to grow runner beans, peas, or cucumber plants as a background to the veggies in the remainder of the bed.

Peas would have the extra benefit of supplying nitrogen to the soil, ensuring a plentiful harvest from nitrogen-hungry plants like cabbage or cauliflower. It is also true that all plants like some nitrogen in their nutritional intake. Thus this strategy would help almost everything.

A single crop

Planting a single crop in a raised bed is normally reserved when you have more than one bed to grow your veggies in. After all, what's the sense of cultivating only one crop unless you're a die-hard pumpkin farmer or can't get enough of a nice cucumber harvest?

Crop rotation is crucial for nutritional value and pest management and concerns like blight and fungal development.

Companion crops are vegetables that get along well with other vegetables, such as onions, carrots, and lettuce, or spinach, onions, and brassicas since their nutritional demands are comparable. Still, their root systems receive nutrients at separate levels and are not in direct conflict.

This is a fantastic concept for pest management and less weeding. The vegetables block out the light to the weeds, and various crops attract different insects, helping restrict the insects' spread.

Crops that do not get along, such as Alliums (onions and garlic) and peas and bean crops, are known as antagonist crops. Beetroot, for example, gets along with most plants and may therefore be planted effectively alongside onions or leeks.

Mixed crop examples

If you just have one raised bed and want to experiment with several vegetable kinds to produce a decent mixed yield, consider the following planting regime:

Tall plants at the rear, supported by permanent support of some type when necessary.

If the climate permits, this might be planted with tomatoes, peas, runner beans, or cucumbers.

Sweet corn might also be utilized here, along with lettuce, to take advantage of the corn's shade. Any low-lying crop, such as carrots, beets, or parsnips, might be planted in front of the raised bed.

If peppers are your primary crop, you may put spinach in between the pepper plants. Similarly to the lettuce and corn examples, the spinach will benefit from and thrive in the shade given by the peppers.

Suppose you live in a colder region, like the UK; you may try covering a piece of your raised bed with a frame like the one shown before and wrapping it with polythene. This will allow you to grow tomatoes, cucumber plants, and perhaps some sweet peppers, which are so costly to purchase at the grocery!

To get the most out of a mixed crop, consider the various veggies' demands in terms of sunshine hours and nutritional requirements. As previously noted, planting veggies with diverse root systems is an excellent idea.

Planting deep-rooted veggies like carrots or parsnips allow you to pair them with shallow-rooted plants like beetroot, lettuce, and arugula (rocket) for a healthy diet.

Maintaining and Growing Plants

Healthy plants, as previously said, are less vulnerable to diseases and pests than not. I aim to maintain my plants as healthy as possible so that they can battle illnesses more effectively. Keeping your plants healthy will aid in their immune system's development. Here are a few pointers to keep your plants healthy and prepared to defend themselves against illnesses.

1. Make that they are adequately fed and hydrated.

2. Create an atmosphere in the garden that will attract beneficial insects and predators. This may attract animals, which can assist in eliminating lesser pests. Ladybugs and lacewings, for example, eat on aphids, whereas birds and hedgehogs graze on slugs.

3. You may use biological controls, like nematodes, to battle snails on hostas or vine weevils in containers.

4. Choose plant species that are more resistant to certain illnesses, such as carrot species that are more resistant to carrot flies than others.

5. I am among those farmers who feel that cultivating certain plants near others may have reciprocal advantages for both plants. This is often referred to as companion planting. Planting carrots and onions together, for example, may bring advantages to both plants. Onion flies are put off by the scent of carrots, while the smell of onion puts carrot flies off.

6. Plant your plants to allow air to flow freely around the raised bed. To remove any fallen leaves or rotten fruits from the floor, I use a little rake. You should be on the lookout for contaminated material and delete it as soon as you see it.

a. Where will my raised bed garden be located?

Plants and vegetables cannot thrive without sunshine for long. It is a necessary component of their nutrition. The more sunlight there is, the more likely your plants will thrive. Plants need around eight hours of sunshine every day on average. As a result, your site choice is heavily influenced by where your yard gets the most sunshine.

Another factor to consider when deciding where to put your raised bed gardens is the kind of soil in your yard. While you may bring in a lot of compost soil from outside, you must first determine if the earth in your location is suitable for such an operation. This test will assist in saving expenses and make integration easier. So, if you discover that your yard has a considerable volume of soil capable of supporting plant life, it would be a pity not to utilize them. Please ensure that the soil from your yard is completely free of weeds, grasses, and debris that will not restrict plant development before planting inside the frames.

Purchasing huge quantities of dirt will suffice if you have a significant number of besteads. They are measured in cubic feet, cubic yards, and cubic meters. When making your purchase, ask for around 60% topsoil, 30% compost, and 10% potting soil, including critical plant nutrients in perlite, vermiculite, and peat moss.

There are additional choices to consider if acquiring high-quality soil is difficult. A combination of equal parts compost and potting soil will work wonders.

CHAPTER 9

Crop Rotation and Planting Techniques

Crop rotation is critical in raised beds to minimize the soil's accumulation of pests and illnesses. Because you're using raised beds, these will be modest at first, but if you produce the same crop year after year in the same bed, you'll run into issues as pests and diseases that target that crop accumulate.

Crop rotation is essential for effective vegetable production since it reduces pests and illnesses and helps guarantee that the soil keeps crucial nutrients and micro-organisms that are helpful to your plants. Succession planting can benefit the soil while still getting more out of your veggie allotment!

Crop rotation is entirely natural and has been performed by farmers for thousands of years because it is essential for maintaining soil quality and interrupting insect lifecycles. However, keep in mind that this only applies to annual plants and not perennials such as asparagus, fruit trees, and so on. These remain in the same location year after year, but you must cultivate the soil, and many people relocate them after they have outlived their usefulness or have reached the end of their lives. During a growth season, applying manure or fertilizer once or twice is frequently enough to keep these permanent plants happy.

Crop rotation reduces the severity and frequency of diseases such as tomato or potato blight, onion/leek rust, and many others, as well as crop-specific pests. Because you do not cultivate the same crop in the same soil season after season, illnesses do not have a chance to accumulate. Some pests and illnesses may survive in the soil for many years, and by rotating your crops, you can guarantee that these pests die off before they can establish themselves.

I know that many of us have a plan, but once we start planting, everything goes out the window because you discover you have an excellent germination rate and plenty of seedlings, people send you plants, you discover fascinating new species to grow, and so on. Crop rotation, on the other hand, can assist in maintaining the soil in your vegetable plot healthy and limit the number of difficulties you experience. Your raised beds make it extremely simple for you to plan and maintain crop rotation. I have a broad planting strategy and will interplant additional crops as needed. Because I practice companion planting, my plants often alternate with herbs, onions, or garlic. However, if any of these plants get ill, I do not replant them in that bed for many years.

The first step is to divide your vegetable plot into several zones, which is simple with raised beds since each raised bed grows one or two varieties of plants. Instead of planting onions and brassicas in the same raised bed (both of which are distinct vegetable families for crop rotation), you would fill the bed with onions. You may plant a few onions as companion plants in the bed, but if you see any indications of illness, stop growing the onions in that area for a number of years. The following year, you would avoid growing any onion family members in that plot and instead plant another sort of crop. Onions are not planted in that bed again until year four; ideally, because of space constraints, year three is more probable.

In a perfect scenario, you'd keep the bed fallow for a year to enable it to relax, absorb nutrients, and disperse bugs. However, in the actual world, most of us consider it to be a waste of excellent growing area, and we are much more likely to utilize the bed but reinforce it with some lovely compost (which most people do every year anyway). If you're planning to leave a bed fallow, spread green manure to keep the weeds at bay and the soil nourished.

You must be methodical in your crop rotation, and I have found that drawing a graphic of your raised bed garden (on the computer and then printing it off) and writing the year on the diagram works best. Then write down what you're planting and where you're putting it, update it at the end of the season to reflect what you really planted, and save it someplace secure. Over the following several years, you may return to this graphic to help you plan your crop rotation planting. It is much more trustworthy than attempting to recall what you planted where three years later! It also keeps an excellent record of everything you've planted and allows you to monitor your triumphs and failures over time. Certain plants may do better in certain beds owing to soil quality, shade, sun, and a variety of other variables.

For crop rotation reasons, vegetables are often divided into four categories:

1. Carrots, potatoes, chicory, artichokes, beets, sal-sify, and parsnips

2. Broccoli, cabbage, kale, turnips, swede, Brussels sprouts, and cauliflower are examples of brassicas.

3. Peas and beans are legumes.

4. Salad crops and other veggies like onions, garlic, leeks, and so on.

None of these crops should be cultivated in the same bed year after year since it depletes the soil of essential nutrients and invites pests and illnesses. Crop rotation is generally unnecessary if you change your raised bed soil yearly; however, most people will not attend this expenditure.

This implies that no plants from the same group should be grown in the same bed for more than a year. So, if you plant cauliflowers in one of your raised beds, you cannot grow swedes or broccoli there the following year; it must be a different crop.

If you've developed a diagram, decide what you're going to plant where, and then rotate your plants one bed anti-clockwise (as is customary) the following year. As long as you don't have two veggies from the same group in neighboring beds, this works. This enables the soil to recuperate, and the legumes will deposit nitrogen in the soil, promoting the growth of your brassicas.

Interplanting

This excellent planting method allows you to grow numerous crops from a single raised bed. It is also known as inter-cropping. This is a terrific method to increase your output and make the most of your raised beds.

This entails growing short-season veggies in between long-season ones. Plant out your tomatoes, which take a long time to grow, and plant vegetables that mature quickly in between, such as spinach, lettuce, radishes, and so on.

These veggies are collected and completed before the main crop plant matures and crowd them out. The major crop plants and the short-season vegetables are planted out at their typical spacing but in between the main crop. Many people will plant lettuce and spinach between their peppers, tomatoes, and eggplants since the primary crop plants focus on building a root system early in the season, while the brief season plants need the top six inches or so of soil. Sowing radishes with your carrots or parsnips is an excellent idea since the radishes sprout rapidly and will designate the row of the slow germination carrots.

Short-season plants develop fast and shade out weeds, allowing the soil to retain moisture and functioning as a barrier or repellent to many pests, making it difficult for them to locate the primary crop plants.

Sweetcorn is another common crop for interplanting, with some people planting pumpkin plants at the base to cover the ground and prevent weeds. This strategy, known as the three sisters method, which also includes growing climbing beans, works, and you will hear about it. The disadvantage of this strategy is that the corn develops before the pumpkins, so you may have to carefully tiptoe past the pumpkins to harvest the corn, but if you don't mind that, this is a terrific way to make excellent use of space.

Don't simply disregard the empty area between your major crop and the slow-developing plants you've planted. Use it to cultivate short-season crops and increase your output significantly!

Succession Planting

This technique solves the issue of an overabundance of vegetables that many gardeners confront. When you grow a row of lettuce plants, they all mature within a week or two of each other, and you end up with more lettuce than you can reasonably utilize. Consequently, most of it bolts and becomes inedible, ending up in the compost heap. Either that, or you're giving veggies away to everyone you know (I used to bring them to work and leave them on reception for anybody to take!).

Using the succession planting approach, you can maintain a consistent supply of short-season vegetables throughout the growing season while avoiding excess tissue.

Planting a small patch of the short-season veggie every two to three weeks during the growing season is more common than planting a large patch all at once. Plants suited for succession planting include carrots, beets, green onions, cilantro, radishes, basils, arugula, spinach, and lettuce. Plants are gathered as they age, and when they are depleted, the following planting should be ready to harvest. This strategy also ensures that if one planting fails due to weather or pests, you will not lose your whole harvest.

For example, if you plant one-eighth of a teaspoon of lettuce seeds every two weeks, you will have a consistent supply throughout the growing season. One of the most common issues a gardener may confront is an abundance of food. It's good if you have relatives and friends to offer it to, but too much produce may be daunting.

This strategy obviously does not work for longer-season veggies since they take so long to develop. If not utilized immediately after maturation, they are often kept or frozen.

Trap Crops

This is an excellent planting approach that includes the planting of a sacrifice crop. Garden pests are drawn to this crop, which you remove and kill once affected, reducing the pest's reproducing population. If you live in a region where certain pests are a problem, this might be a viable technique for producing crops that bugs would otherwise destroy.

Aphids, for example, like nasturtiums, so put them near your cabbages to keep the aphids away from your harvest.

The sacrifice crop is then covered with a plastic bag, ensuring no pests escape and is destroyed. Pests may be killed by leaving the plant in a sealed bag in the sun or burning it. If you're going to compost it, be sure you bury it in the center of a hot compost pile, otherwise, the bugs will live and escape. I would suggest eliminating the contaminated plant material since most of us do not run compost heaps hot enough to kill the bugs.

Keeping a few of these trap plants away from your crop may increase the number of beneficial insects since the

predators will stay in your vegetable plot and continue
to hunt the pests.

CHAPTER 10

Tips

Raised bed gardens offer several advantages and disadvantages. Also, each garden has an infinite number of materials and crops to choose from. We've previously discussed how you should aim to keep your gardens small or restrict a particular crop to a specific location. Another aspect is the concept of succession planting. Succession planting is a method of increasing the total productivity of your property by planting crops in a specific sequence. For example, if you like both a particular summer plant and a winter plant, you may sow the seeds for the winter plant immediately after harvesting the summer one. This fast-paced gardening approach is designed to optimize your garden and available area. Because of the little constrained space required to put your vegetables in a raised bed garden, this works effectively. To utilize succession planting successfully, you must first understand what crops thrive during certain seasons and then use that information to create a chain that allows you to easily transition your garden from one season to the next.

Raised bed gardens are also ideal for practicing companion planting in addition to succession planting. Companion planting is the practice of carefully growing crops to benefit one another. The widespread practice of growing beans amid corn stalks is one example of this. Each plant benefits the other because the beans absorb nitrogen in the soil, providing additional nutrients for the corn. The corn offers a natural trellis, allowing the beans to grow longer. This is only one example of the many mutuality interactions that may be discovered via companion planting. Companion gardening is also quite effective in a small area. As a consequence, raised bed gardens are ideal places to experiment with companion planting. If you use various species on a bed in a raised bed garden, the crops will grow close to one another. As a result, if your plants share the same area, it is a good idea to attempt to make that shared space work for your plants. This will simplify gardening and help your crops thrive to their maximum potential.

While there are suggested sizes and forms for raised bed gardens, keep in mind that you may install your garden in a variety of locations. Some individuals create bed gardens that are simply big enough to contain a single crop they do not need in great quantities but enjoy at their table. Others place raised bed gardens beside their driveways or on their windowsills. Because the garden may be restricted to a box, there are several strategic locations where you can position your bed. If you like gardening or architecture, you may position your bed to provide an aesthetically pleasing or intriguing aspect to your yard. You may even make your elevated bed tiered by putting a smaller bed in the center of a bigger one. This may be pretty attractive and provide an alternative to the classic raised garden.

Water is essential for a healthy, growing raised bed garden (as it is for all gardens). However, as previously said, raised bed dirt drains faster than regular soil. As a result, many individuals install an irrigation system in their beds before planting. An irrigation system is an excellent tool for ensuring that your plants get enough water. Not only that, but it will significantly simplify your gardening operation. If an irrigation system waters your plants, you will save time by not having to walk around your beds with a hose all the time, making an already simple gardening process even easier and allowing you to focus on planting and harvesting rather than constantly tending to your plants and garden.

Raised bed gardens are ideal for both novice and expert gardeners. They provide an excellent foundation for a new garden and may be used to make the whole gardening process simpler. Many individuals have their own motivations for beginning a raised bed garden, but regardless of the cause, raised bed gardens produce more and bigger plants than regular gardens. This is because the circumstances are typically superior and support potent seed and root growth owing to the spacing and isolated habitat. Furthermore, raised bed gardens are simpler to access, allowing you to properly water and maintain each crop. While the upkeep of a raised bed garden is fundamentally comparable to that of a more typical ground garden, there are several additional advantages to a raised bed garden. A raised bed garden is a terrific addition to any yard or house, regardless of the design or kind of raised bed garden you pick, the materials you want to use, or the location you wind up putting your garden. The majority of the labor is in the actual construction of the bed, but it is well worth it since that small amount of time and energy will pay off immensely.

CHAPTER 11

Growing and Harvesting

Watering Your Garden

You'll need to offer additional irrigation for your garden whether you live in a drought-prone location or in a climate with above-average rainfall. It is advisable to arrange your watering system at the time of planting or shortly after.

Hand-watering using watering cans or a hose may suffice in a small raised bed garden or container garden. However, this needs hands-on attention and work, which you may only want to commit to for part of the gardening season. Furthermore, overhead watering exacerbates fungal infections that flourish in moist and humid circumstances.

Many gardeners choose to use irrigation systems like soaker hoses or drip emitters. Because water is absorbed directly into the soil using these techniques, less water is lost through evaporation. Soaker hoses are ideal for raised beds because they equally saturate the raised bed by leaching water along the length of the line. They look great in beds with closely spaced plants like carrots, beets, lettuce, greens, and onions.

Drip emitter systems are suitable for all sorts of gardening. Every 18 inches, the drip lines drain water. They are simple to install, and you can customize and extend your drip system as your garden grows. Lines connected with discrete "spot" emitters give one water supply per container.

For soaker hoses or drip systems, purchase a cheap timer that can be attached to your water faucet and allows you to control when and how long your plant gets water. Because each system progressively leaches water, it's preferable to leave it on for a few hours for each watering. During peak season, my garden is set to get water from 5:00 a.m. until 7:00 a.m. every 3 to 4 days. My timer includes a "rain delay" feature that lets me postpone the planned watering if we have rain.

In general, most vegetables and herbs in an in-ground or raised bed garden flourish with 1 inch of water each week. Purchasing a rain gauge can assist you in determining when more watering is required.

Because of the well-draining characteristics of container soil, container plants demand more water. Because plants exhibit the same signs of drooping and wilting leaves when overwatered and underwatered, a rain gauge and moisture meter will assist you in assessing water-related concerns throughout the growing season.

Gardening Maintenance

Although no garden will live up to the aspirations of a wide-eyed rookie gardener (no matter what you do, you will have to fight weeds and bugs), the following ideas will help maintain your garden as healthy as possible.

Every day, go around your garden. Checking your garden on a regular basis, even if you are not working in it, allows you to keep an eye on development and any problems. Diseases and pests may quickly take over untended gardens, but early action can reduce the damage.

Pests should be handpicked. Learn about the most common pests, such as aphids, squash bugs, hornworms, bean beetles, cucumber beetles, cabbage worms, and so

on, and handpick any you notice. Try physically removing them before using spray (organic or not). Grab some
gardening gloves and a pail of water (with a splash of dish
detergent to reduce surface tension) and drop the bugs in.

Don't exterminate an insect you can't identify. The majority of the insects in your garden are either useful or harmless. If you're unsure, leave it alone; many helpful insects
feed on harmful ones. An Internet search and Facebook
gardening communities where knowledgeable gardeners can assist you in identifying an insect will be useful.
Ladybugs, lacewings, syrphid flies or hoverflies, ground
beetles, assassin bugs, and spiders are all beneficial insects.

ADD flowers. Add flowers and allow bolted plants to
blossom to attract beneficial insects. Cosmos, calendula,
nasturtium, sunflowers, yarrow, zinnia, and alyssum are
all excellent additions. Bolted lettuce, arugula, carrots,
and onions produce blossoms that attract a slew of helpful insects, as do herbs like oregano, parsley, cilantro, and
thyme. These helpful insects will keep many pest insects
at bay if provided with an appropriate home. I seldom
have to spray for aphids, for example, since ladybugs,
lacewings, and syrphid flies take care of them.

Mulch. Don't put off mulching. When the plants are approximately 6 inches tall, apply a 2-inch layer of mulch to prevent weeds and save moisture.

Weed on a regular basis. Even with mulch, some weed shoots emerge. Put weeding on your schedule at least once a week. It's considerably more difficult to keep up with weeds after they've grown out of control.

Water first thing in the morning. Water in the early hours, whether you hand-water or utilize a drip irrigation system. This provides the plants with the moisture they need at the optimal moment while also limiting evaporation and reducing the development of fungal infections that are frequent with nighttime watering.

If required, fertilize. Many new gardens do not need additional fertilization at first, but as plants absorb nutrients from the soil, more fertilizer might be beneficial. Fish emulsion is an efficient organic and low-dose nitrogen source. This aids plants in their early stages of growth in developing the leaves required for photosynthesis. Too much nitrogen may cause fruiting plants to produce an abundance of foliage but few fruits. Skip the nitrogen fertilizer if your plants are developing quickly. However, if they seem stunted, this low-dose type of nitrogen may be beneficial. In my raised bed gardens, I use fish emulsion for my fruiting plants every two weeks until they begin to bloom.

Remove unhealthy foliage. Fungal infections are the most frequent plant diseases. These do not immediately destroy the plant, but if left uncontrolled, they may. Early blight is generally indicated by yellow leaves at the bottom of tomato plants, while powdery mildew is indicated by white powder on squash and cucumber leaves. Remove diseased leaves and stems as soon as possible and dispose of them in the garbage (not compost). You may prune up to 25% of a plant's leaves. When sickness is detected early, it may be contained.

Vertical plants should be trained to grow up trellises. Plants like beans and peas typically train themselves, while cucumbers and vining tomatoes need assistance. Wrap cucumber vines in a zigzag manner around the trellis every few days. Lift tomato vines and place them on the appropriate rung of a tomato cage or tie them to a trellis. It is critical to maintaining the vines spread apart for adequate ventilation when training them.

These little maintenance procedures can maintain your landscape in the best possible condition. However, keep in mind that when utilizing organic approaches, it takes time for healthy insect populations and soil to develop.

Expect growth rather than perfection throughout the first season.

Common Pests and Problems, and What to Do About Them

Throughout the growing season, each organic garden will confront various issues and pests, and you won't know which ones you'll encounter until you start cultivating. These are a few of the most prevalent problems.

Tomatoes with early blight or Septoria leaf spot. These fungi cause yellowing leaves to appear at the base of tomato plants. Early blight may resemble a bullseye, with outside yellow rings darkening to brown in the center. Septoria leaf spot appears as several brown spots on the leaves and usually occurs later in the season. When the leaves aren't damp, cut off and discard any afflicted stems. During wet seasons, you may need to do this on a regular basis to keep it under control.

Powdery mildew is a kind of mildew. Powdery mildew is a fungal disease that appears as white powder on the tips of leaves and is most frequent on squash, zucchini, and cucumbers. If not controlled, it will grow up the plant, preventing photosynthesis and subsequent fruit production. If you find it early, you may remove up to 25% of the plant's damaged leaves. If it doesn't work, combine one teaspoon of baking soda with 1-quart water and spray damaged and unaffected leaves once a week.

The rot of the blossom end. This black rotting patch, which is most frequent on tomatoes, emerges when the flower falls off the fruit. Squash, melons, and peppers are also susceptible. Although this problem is caused by a plant's failure to absorb calcium from the soil, merely adding calcium is rarely an effective treatment. Most soils have enough calcium present (a soil test can confirm this); the issue typically lies in inconsistent irrigation or out-of-balance pH. Water plants on a regular basis, particularly throughout the blooming and fruiting seasons. Whether this doesn't work, obtain a soil test to see if a calcium deficiency or a pH imbalance is to cause.

Pollination needs to be improved. When a fruit stops developing and starts to decay, it is typically due to a lack of pollination. This problem is most common in squash, zucchini, cucumbers, and melons. Cross-pollinating plants can only produce fruit with pollinators such as bees. Hand pollination may be required. Locate the male flower (the one without a fruit forming at the base) and use a cotton swab to transfer the pollen from its stamen to the female bloom (the one with a fruit at the base). These flowers only bloom once a day, generally in the morning, so you'll have to get up early every day.

Aphids. Aphids are tiny, pear-shaped insects that cluster on new growth of many plants, including tomatoes and peppers, particularly early in the season. Spraying should be avoided since most insecticidal soaps also kill the larvae of ladybugs, lacewings, and syrphid flies, which dine on aphids. Instead, add worm castings to the roots of the plants and thoroughly water them. Worm castings include chitinase, an enzyme that aphids cannot digest. Aphids die after sucking plant liquids containing chitinase.

Worms. Cabbage worms, tomato hornworms, armyworms, and other worms may quickly defoliate your food plants. If handpicking isn't enough, treat afflicted crops with the organic insecticide Bacillus thuringiensis, being cautious not to spray any blooms. A floating row cover might also be used to protect sensitive crops (broccoli, cabbage, kale, and lettuce) from the moths that deposit the eggs that hatch into these worms.

Beetles. Squash bugs, stinkbugs, Japanese bean beetles, Mexican bean beetles, cucumber beetles, and other insects are among the most challenging pests to eradicate. Organic alternatives are limited since deterrents that may influence these insects would also kill beneficial beetles like ground beetles and ladybugs. The best way to manage these pests is to handpick adults and remove egg clusters. Removing infected plants and performing crop rotation is also beneficial in future seasons.

When it comes to difficulties in an organic garden, less is more. The greatest defense is early hand removal of sick plants and pests. Accept some damage and remember that the richer the soil is, the stronger the plants will be, allowing them to resist more insect and disease damage throughout the season.

CHAPTER 12

Plant Profiles

ASPARAGUS

Asparagus officinalis is a medicinal plant.

Asparagus dislikes competing with weeds, so keep your bed clean. Asparagus plants may survive for 15 years or more, producing every year once established.

Asparagaceae is a family of plants.

Growing Plant in early spring, 4 to 6 weeks before the last frost.

Zones 3–8; due to the variation of these zones, choose the variety most suited to yours.

12 to 18 inch space between

Plant seedlings (crowns) the first year and harvest lightly the following spring.

Indoor Planting Starting: not suggested since your harvest period will be one year longer; instead, utilize plant crowns (dormant roots of year-old plants) acquired from a seed provider.

Outdoor planting should begin as soon as your raised bed can be worked.

Watering: water on a regular basis.

Starting Point: full sun, partial shade

Plant crowns in an 8-inch-deep trench before transplanting. Cover the roots with 1 to 2 inches of dirt and spread them out. As the plants develop, you will fill up the trench with dirt.

Before planting crowns, add lime and fertilizer. Asparagus prefers a pH of around 7.

Growing Keep asparagus hydrated the first year, particularly during dry spells. Avoid overwatering. The roots dislike being extremely damp.

Mulch extensively to keep weeds at bay.

Harvest the spears before the tops sprout fern-like leaves. At ground level, make a cut.

Problems

Remove the asparagus beetle by hand.

Fungicide should be used to treat fusarium wilt.

BASIL

Basilicum ocimum

Try planting large-leaf basil for wraps and purple basil
for a focal point in your yard.

Lamiaceae is a family of plants.

Growing Spring and late spring are the seasons.

Zones three through ten

12 to 18 inch spacing

50 to 90 days from seed to harvest

Indoor seedlings should be started 6 to 8 weeks before the last frost.

Earliest Outdoor Planting: after threat of frost; ground should be 60 degrees Fahrenheit

Watering: 1 inch of water each week is required through-out the development cycle.

Starting Point: full sun

When planting directly in the garden, cover seeds with 14 inch of dirt.

Growing

Basil should never be let to dry out. Watering on a reg-ular basis is ideal. Pinch off the plant tips as they begin to blossom to generate bushy plants.

Harvesting Remove as many leaves as you want.

Problems

Choose types that are slow to bolt if you are growing basil in a warm climate.

BEET

B. vulgaris

Beet greens and roots may be eaten. They may be roasted, pickled, grilled, or boiled, and they store nicely in the freezer.

Chenopodiaceae is a family of plants.

Growing Seasons: in warmer regions, early spring or late autumn; in colder climates, late spring or early fall.

Zones three through ten

12 inch space between

50 to 60 days from seed to harvest

Indoor Planting Starting: not recommended

Outdoor planting should begin as soon as your raised bed can be handled in milder climes; in frost-free places, seed in the autumn.

Watering frequency: 1 inch per week

Starting Point: full sun, partial shade

Planting: Beets dislike acidic soil and prefer a pH range of 6 to 7.

Growing

Too much nitrogen causes the tips to develop faster than the roots.

Harvesting

When beet greens are 4 to 5 inches long, harvest them. Harvest the roots when they are 1 to 3 inches in diameter.

Problems

Handpick and destroy infected leaves using a leaf miner.

Keep water away from the green tips of the leaves.

BELL PEPPER

Annuum Capsicum

Plant bell peppers in places where you previously planted eggplant, peppers, potatoes, or tomatoes.

Solanaceae is a family of plants.

Growing Seasons: early spring in warm regions; late spring to early summer in colder climates.

Zones three through ten

14 to 16 inch space between

65 to 70 days from seed to harvest

Indoor Planting Starting: 8 to 10 weeks before the last frost; seeds may be sown straight in the garden in the Deep South.

Outdoor planting should begin as soon as the risk of the final frost has passed.

Watering frequency: 1 to 2 inches per week

Starting Point: full sun

Growing

If the plant receives too much nitrogen, it will produce more leaves than peppers.

Harvesting

Instead than picking peppers off the stem, cut them off. Peppers gain taste as they age.

Problems

Aphids: Use natural soap and water to remove them.

Blossom end rot: This issue generally clears up on its own. Cut \sout the afflicted piece and consume the remainder of the pepper.

Cucumber mosaic virus (CMV): Remove sick plants and dispose of them; prepare a new planting area for the next year.

BROCCOLI

Brassica oleracea var. italica

If you reside in a warm region, growing broccoli in the autumn is better since it thrives in chilly temperatures.

Brassicaceae is a family of plants.

Growing Spring, autumn, and chilly weather

Zones 3–10; if you live in a hotter area, sow heat-tolerant seeds.

Spacing: 18 to 24 inches in 3 foot rows

45 to 60 days from seed to harvest

Indoor Planting Starting time: 7 to 9 weeks before the final spring frost; provide seedlings with 14 to 16 hours of light each day using fluorescent lights.

Outdoor planting should begin two weeks before the final spring frost; in the autumn, 85 to 100 days before the first frost in warm areas.

Watering should be mild and even; only the roots, not the leaves, should be watered.

Starting Location: full light; plants can tolerate moderate shade, but will develop more slowly.

Planting: Broccoli enjoys temperatures ranging from 64 to 73 degrees Fahrenheit. It can be sown in soil temperatures as low as 40 degrees Fahrenheit.

Growing

Broccoli can withstand frost. Because of its weak root system, it is best to utilize mulch rather than a cultivator.

If you find yellow blooms, pluck the heads and utilize them right away since they are little beyond their peak. With a pair of garden shears, cut the center head of each broccoli plant to promote development on the side stems, which will continue to generate heads for many weeks.

Problems

Aphids: To get rid of them, use insecticidal soap or a strong spray of water.

Cabbage worms: physically remove them or use row coverings to keep them away.

CABBAGE

Brassica oleracea var. capitata

Some cabbage types produce blooms. These plants' leaves are edible, however they are mainly used as a garnish. Examine your seed packs to ensure that you have edible cabbage leaves.

Brassicaceae is a family of plants.

Growing Plant in early spring and late autumn.

Zones three through ten

12 to 18 inch space between

50 to 60 days from seed to harvest

Indoor Planting Beginning: 6–8 weeks before the last frost

Outdoor planting should begin as soon as your raised bed can be worked.

Watering: keep plants well-watered during dry spells.

Starting Point: full sun

Planting: Plants may tolerate a mild frost.

Growing

Cabbage's root system is shallow. When weeding or cultivating, avoid injuring it.

Harvesting

When the heads are hard, harvest them.

Problems

Cabbage aphids may be removed using an insecticidal soap or a vigorous spray of water.

Cabbage worms: physically remove them or use row coverings to keep them at bay.

Remove the afflicted plants from the clubroot.

Cutworms must be physically removed.

CANTALOUPE

Cucumis melo var. cantalupensis

Cantaloupes are often grown on the ground rather than on a trellis since they "slide" off the vine when mature.

Cucurbitaceae family

Growing Seasons: Early spring in warmer regions; late spring to early summer in colder climes.

Zones three through ten

Dimensions: 36 to 48 inches apart

70 to 85 days from seed to harvest

Indoor seed starting: 3 to 4 weeks before planting, however direct sowing is preferred.

Outdoor planting should begin as soon as frost risk has gone.

Watering frequency: 1 to 2 inches per week

Starting Point: full sun

Growing

Melons have a shallow root system that should be avoided while weeding or cultivating.

Use a lot of mulch if you're growing melons in the ground so they don't sit in the dirt.

Harvesting

Melons that are ripe will "slide" off the vine. You won't have to apply much pressure to get them to release.

They are ripe when they begin to smell like a melon.

Problems

Aphids: To get rid of them, use insecticidal soap or a strong spray of water.

Powdery mildew: Spray plants with a solution of 2 to 3 teaspoons white vinegar per gallon of water to kill powdery mildew.

Squash bugs: In the morning and later in the day, remove eggs from the underside of leaves.

Use a fungicide to treat wilt disease.

CARROT

Daucus carot

Plant carrots every several weeks for continuous harvests.

Apiaceae is a family of plants.

Growing Seasons: spring and autumn, depending on location; check your time zone for exact dates.

Zones three through ten

3 to 4 inch spacing in rows 1 to 2 feet apart

50 to 80 days from seed to harvest

Indoor Planting Plant immediately in the garden since they dislike being transferred.

Outdoor planting should begin after the threat of severe frost has passed; in frost-free locations, plant in the autumn.

Watering: maintain wet but not saturated; drip irrigation is preferable; do not water foliage

Starting Point: full sun

Seedlings should not be started inside. Direct planting.

Planting Instructions: Cover seeds with 12 inch of soil. Plant them in deep, loose soil to allow the roots to develop.

Growing

All that is required is weeding and watering. During the growing cycle, carrots need 1 inch of water every week. They should not be grown on clay soil.

Harvesting is as simple as twisting and pulling the roots, taking care not to rip the tops off.

To store the carrots, clean them and trim the green tips to just above the root.

Problems

Aster yellows disease is caused by the aster leafhopper and results in shorter tops and hairy roots. Use a sticky trap purchased at hardware shops to control the insect and keep this illness at bay.

Fusarium: When carrots are left in the ground beyond their prime, this fungus causes dry rot of the root. Pick carrots at maturity to avoid fusarium.

CHIVES

Allium schoenoprasum

Chives make an excellent focal point in a garden bed and a tasty complement to many dishes. Divide clumps every 3 to 4 years for the highest output and healthiest plants.

Amaryllidaceae is a family of flowers.

Growing Spring and late spring are the seasons.

Zones three through ten

3 to 4 inch space between

80 to 90 days from seed to harvest

Indoor Planting Beginning: 8 to 10 weeks before the final spring frost.

Outdoor planting should begin as soon as there is a risk of severe frost.

Watering: carefully water seedlings after planting; plants need around 1 inch of water each week.

Starting Point: full sun

Seeding: Seeds may be started inside or planted directly in the ground.

Plant seedlings with plenty of area for the root ball before transplanting.

Planting: Cover seeds with 14 inch of soil in the garden.

Growing

The only upkeep required is weeding and watering.

Clip plants to 1 inch above the ground for harvesting. The tips will regenerate.

Problems Chives are normally pest-free.

CILANTRO

Coriandrum sativum

Cilantro may be obtained as cilantro (the fresh herb) or coriander (the dried herb) (the seed). Harvest cilantro plants after the green leaves appear, but before the plants blossom. Harvest coriander seeds when they become grayish-brown.

Apiaceae is a family of plants.

Growing Spring and early summer are the seasons.

Zones three through ten

10 to 14 inch spacing

60 to 90 days from seed to harvest

Indoor Planting Starting: 6 to 8 weeks before the final frost threat.

Outdoor planting should begin as soon as frost is no longer a threat.

Watering: 1 inch of water each week is required.

Starting Point: full sun

Plant seeds inside 6 to 8 weeks before the final frost.

Planting Instructions: Cover seeds with 14 inch of soil. If you want a constant crop, plant every three weeks.

Growing

Cilantro need one inch of water per week. Fertilize not.

Harvesting

Cut to 2 inches above the ground with scissors.

Problems

Keep the soil wet to prevent wilting.

CHAPTER 13

Raised Bed Maintenance

Even the most basic Raised Bed gardens will need some maintenance at some point. Upkeep of the removal system covers everything from measuring and fixing nutrient concentrations to flushing out the machine on a regular basis, as well as the occasional cleaning of strands and reservoirs.

MANAGEMENT OF THE NUTRITIONAL SOLUTION

There are several methods for caring for a Raised Bed nutrition solution. Crop selection, window proportions, garden design and style, and personal preference will determine the orientation plan for the Raised Bed garden. If it means sacrificing growing pace or harvest quality, I typically choose the alternative that takes the shortest duration. However, in order to optimize development, you should tighten up on your nutrition. The following guidance approaches are organized by the time and effort that they may need.

Least effort: SET IT AND FORGET IT

Build the reservoir with all of the appropriate fertilizer rates per gallon written down on the compost bag/bottle. Correct the pH if it is significantly over the target range or not. Allow the harvest to cultivate until it is ready to crop or until the water level is low enough for plants to obtain safe access to the nutrient solution. This strategy may work well for leafy greens in floating raft systems and may work in other systems if they have a large enough reservoir to accommodate growing plants. Using this low-effort strategy, I've produced a surprising number of beautiful plants. This orientation style may cause issues when used with plants that have extended development cycles, such as berries, cucumbers, peppers, and many blooming plants. Try out the best strategy if you want to employ theoretical work while also growing plants for longer before maturity.

SMALL EFFORT: top-off

This method is similar to forget and set; however, when the water level declines, the grower merely adds water to maintain the previous quantity. This approach may thicken the nutrient concentration at the reservoir over time, and nutritional deficits may occur during the harvest. This strategy may work for rapid plants with modest nutritional needs, such as micro-greens, leafy greens, and a few herbaceous plants. This approach may work for multiple larger plants depending on the equipment; nevertheless, there is a risk of diluting the nutrient solution, particularly when using a small reservoir.

MAKE AN EFFORT: TOP OFF AND CHANGE

The most common method of maintaining a nutrient solution in a Raised Bed garden is to fill the reservoir as described in the preceding technique, then add additional fertilizer to the pool to maintain the desired EC.

Please see the appendix for further information, such as target ECs for common Raised Bed plants. After adding compost to get the desired EC, the gardener adjusts the pH of the nutrient solution using either an acid (pH down) or a base (pH up) (pH upward). There are several easy-to-use pHs and pH solutions available in growing shops, as well as DIY ones that are, in many circumstances, less optimum yet functional. Some Raised Bed gardeners use vinegar or lemon juice to reduce pH, while others use baking soda. An EC meter, Raised Bed mulch, a measuring cup, a pH meter, pH down and pH adjustments, and a pipette will be required to fill up and modify the clear answer on your system (eyedropper).

FLUSHING

EC is an excellent general nutrition material benchmark for a Raised Bed reservoir. Unfortunately, it does not provide the whole story. Not all essential components were absorbed by plants at the same rate. Some nutrition may accumulate over time, while others will most likely be drained quickly, resulting in an unbalanced nutritional treatment. Massive commercial Raised Bed farms send water samples to testing facilities to get specified levels of each nutrient from the reservoir. In addition, the farmer corrects the fertilizer inputs as a result. Such fertilizer modifications need complex chemistry and even a thorough understanding of a harvest's nutritional requirements. The far-easier alternative is to implement a Raised Bed program.

Flushing eliminates the present nutrient solution and rehydrates the system with fresh water before adding new fertilizer. The occurrence of flushing is affected by a variety of factors, including harvest, environment, strategy, fertilizer, and water quality. Most fishermen succeed by using the following strategies to improve flush consistency: "Flush a reservoir once the volume of water placed into it is more equivalent to the size of this reservoir." For example, a 40-gallon reservoir contributes 5 gallons to evapotranspiration (plant transpiration and reservoir evaporation) per day.

Every day, the grower adds 5 liters to the reservoir to compensate for water loss from the lake. The grower adds 40 gallons (8 weeks x 5 gallons 40 gallons) to the same water level at the main reservoir measurement after seven days. The reservoir should be fed every eight days by the farmer. This suggestion is quite cautious, and many planters may often flush when using standard raised bed fertilizers. This idea is useful, but only as a general guideline. The water released from the Raised Bed System does not have to go down the drain. Many fishermen still use the earlier fertilizer treatment to water their potted plants, raised beds, yards, or even trees. A traditional garden is an excellent friend for your garden; also, it may be property for ancient house solutions, such as plant plants and substrates.

CLEANING

Raised Bed farmers may sterilize their crops using a variety of services and products. Dish soap is typically the safest and most easy solution. Some additional options for hobby Raised Bed farmers include household bleach (use 1/2 to one ounce per gallon of water), isopropyl alcohol (70 percent or more moderate), and hydrogen peroxide (3 percent is usually adequate; higher concentrations are available, but they must be handled with caution, read and read product labels).

Conclusion

Now that you have all the necessary information, it is time to start. During the day, go around your available area to pick a sunny spot. Decide on the size and dimensions of your raised bed once you've selected where it will go. Make a list of everything you'll need, from the soil, compost, and other components to the frames. After you've set up your bed and filled it with dirt, it's time to focus on the plants. Choose the vegetables you wish to cultivate based on my recommendations. If you wish to grow plants from seeds, you will need to prepare ahead of time since they will take time to mature into seedlings ready to be put outdoors in your box. Alternatively, you may buy seedlings to put straight into your raised beds.

The key to practically raised bed gardening is a well-planned garden and selecting the appropriate soil. These gardening techniques are not new; they have been used in some form or another for centuries. Raised bed gardens are becoming more popular in the United States. Specific technical components of planning may differ from place to region, but the basics are almost universal. If used correctly, these strategies may result in considerably higher output rates (as much as 4 to 10 times higher, according to some estimates) than traditional gardening methods on average rich terrain.

One of the essential aspects contributing to the effectiveness and efficiency of raised beds is that crops can grow in precisely the correct sort of soil - deep, rich, and loose enough to provide a greater output rate. This is feasible because the general state of the setup is conducive to appropriate soil drainage and aeration, allowing plant roots to penetrate deeper.

Aside from that, maintaining a raised bed garden is relatively simple. Removing weeds and rubble takes very little time, allowing you to concentrate on other vital activities like watering the plants. Because the gardener is constantly standing in the route, the plants are never in danger of being trampled. Unlike conventional gardening techniques, you may focus your soil amendment and improvement efforts on the beds, not the walkway. This helps you save both resources and time.

Raised bed gardening is appealing since it needs no particular maintenance or attention. The only things you'll ever have to worry about are watering the plants, planting and harvesting them at the appropriate times, and weeding the garden on a regular basis. When you harvest a plant, fill the empty spot with compost and replant.

The next step for you is to organize a stroll around your possible raised bed garden space. Remember, if you have enough light, excellent soil, and lots of water, you'll be OK.

Best wishes and happy harvesting!

www.ingramcontent.com/pod-product-compliance
Lightning Source LLC
LaVergne TN
LVHW010633200726

843507LV00011B/1691